# THE LAYERS OF LIFE

## Thoughts on Nature, Living, and Self-Reliance

### John D. McCann

# The Layers Of Life

## Thoughts on Nature, Living and Self-Reliance

## John D. McCann

ISBN-978-0-9905006-2-9

I dedicate this book to Denise,
my beautiful wife and best friend

# TABLE OF CONTENTS

# Winter's Unique Beauty

# Winter's Unique Beauty

Winter is a season of frosty, frigid, and snowy weather resulting in many additional tasks of exertion and drudgery. But, if one can overlook and disregard these bothersome inconveniences, and look beyond them, they will discover a beauty difficult to replicate in other seasons.

A field blanketed with snow, as if enveloped by a white down comforter, conceals the features of topography while insulating that which lies beneath, resulting in a new landscape much different than during other seasons. Shadows are longer and prevaricate and exaggerate the true stature of shapes being replicated. Although the season is harsh, there is a softness to the surroundings.

The woods stripped of its foliage, like the curtains from a window, appear larger, more spacious, and easier to navigate. The bright, vibrant, colors are gone. But a new pallet of peaceful and neutral tones and shades provide a scene reminiscent of a black and white photo, where shadows and tints tell the story.

A snow covered branch resembles an outstretched arm covered by a diminutive quilt to shield and insulate it from a cold gust of wind. Drifts of snow can create forms that disguise or misrepresent what actually lies beneath. A ramble through a field of snow only inches deep can suddenly deepen considerably with little forewarning that a drift is in your path.

There is a peacefulness about winter. Yet there is a dichotomy between the silence and the sounds. The silence of winter is almost a sound within itself. Sometimes the tranquility of the quiescence deceives one into almost believing that the absence of sound is a sound. Much like the sound of no sound you hear when you place your ear close to a large shell. And yet the real sounds are clear and crisp. The mere crunch of frozen snow beneath your feet can be resounding in the encompassing quietude.

There is no one who, at some point in their life, has not been in awe of the spectacle of the snow flake. Each one different, yet similar, accumulating in a blanket of white. Who has not had one land on an eye lash or be caught by an outstretched tongue? The enchanting delight of falling snow flakes can entrance the young and old alike.

The ice formations of winter are a delight to behold. The formation of a single icicle, created by the simple freezing of dripping water. It dangles like a translucent dagger, prepared to pierce the snow beneath when dislodged from its berth of origin. A precipice can become a sculpture of ice as layer upon layer of frozen leakage builds upon itself forming a hue of blue, changing constantly as the overlapping coatings progress. Streams are transformed from a brisk movement of water to a stationary carpet of snow covered ice. Although the current continues below, the surface above becomes a continuation of the surrounding features.

Life beneath the snow continues. The moles and mice burrow tunnels under the blanket of snow providing a labyrinth of passage much like the subways beneath a city. Plant life. such as the common chickweed, continue their existence and can provide a winter snack if the location beneath the snow is known.

Winter, like all seasons, is a time unto itself. Different, yet splendid, it its own right. It is a time for a unique beauty that only winter can bestow.

# Early Morning Jaunt

# Early Morning Jaunt

At dawn I enter the forest as if her eyes are yet completely open. The new light of day filters delicately through the canopy that protects her; even though the day's new sun has yet to reveal itself. My nostrils take custody of the early morning fragrance of the dew laden earth.

An owl is observed sitting majestically on a large limb, but no movements are witnessed. However, the movements of other awakening inhabitants begin slowly as they move forth to begin another day. A squirrel emerges from its nest, almost appearing to be wiping the sleep from its eyes. It then ambles downward from its tree and across the leaves in such a hushed manner that, if I had not caught the movement with peripheral vision, the moment would have gone unnoticed.

Early morning feeders, a Doe and her fawn, are observed walking in a leisurely, yet guarded manner. As the fawn, stops, stoops, and feeds, the mother watches, as a sentry on duty. They pass with an easy gait, noticing me, but apparently not alarmed, as I stand motionless, only watching.

The sound of fluttering wings provide evidence that a bird has taken early morning flight, but is confirmed only by the sound, as actual observation fails to be captured. Oftentimes, sounds appear to originate from one direction, but the reflection of sound waves through the trees, can cause a false sense of origination. Therefore, flight and identification of the early morning aviator will wait for another day.

Well, the first rays of the morning sun begin to filter through the trees and appear as rays of hope for a new day. Only in the early morning light can one feel as though they are again being reborn, coming to life for the first time, greeting a new day. Experiencing the aroma and quietude gives one a feeling of peacefulness and the forest offers a perceived sense of protection. I will return tomorrow, and with that return, another day of expectation will transpire.

# The Layers Of Life

# The Layers Of Life

I was hiking through the Watkins Glen State Park in western New York and observed the cavernous depths created by the unknown years of water sculpting the earth's surface, creating vast walls. It was like a miniature Grand Canyon, yet more intimate, due to the narrowness and diminutive nature of the meandering precipice.

As I walked and observed the majesty of that scene, I could not help but observe the many layers of the earth's surface, revealed like the layers of an onion. I began to realize that each layer was a time span that lasted for an unspecific amount of time, yet specific things occurred. There were certain weather patterns, animal species, plant life, that may have been different than today. Yet it was the accumulation of time that created the end result.

Later, upon reflection of that hike, I began to realize that the revelation of the layers uncovered by nature could be analogous to the life of man, and the parallels to life on earth. Although life is molded by experiences and can meander in many directions, it continues creating new layers, resulting in the person you become.

We often think of our youth, and remember those things that brought us both happiness and despair. Yet these early events actually create our initial layer. As we grow, additional layers accumulate, and that compilation is created by events, observations, relationships, happiness and hardships.

Like the earth, some surfaces are soft, having been shaped by favorable conditions. Yet other surfaces become hard, as a result of extremes of nature having been cruel and unrelenting. The surface of the earth must submit to those conditions thrust upon her. But man has options. Man can change the direction in which they travel and seek more favorable conditions for life.

I have meet people who have allowed the turmoil's of life to create hardened layers that prevent them from enjoying the pleasurable aspects of life. Yet others, even though enduring unwarranted tribulations, have perpetuated peaceful and gratifying lives. Not all layers of life will be good. But allowing them to settle, and building upon each other, and applying the experience that each layer provides, can result in a strong foundation for further growth. We are the result of our travels, a sum of the whole. We exist through the layers of life.

# Spring - The Awakening

# Spring - The Awakening

It seems only a short time ago that the shell like flowers of the skunk cabbage were poking their heads through the last remnants of snow, like a crustacean breaching the surface of the water. The buckets were being filled with the sweet sap of the sugar maples, draining from the spiles, like a leaking faucet. But now, the door of winter has finally closed and the gates of spring have crept open.

The days get longer and the cold of winter is replaced with a warmth that emanates from the earth and embraces the soul. The scent of the breeze is distinctly different and new, and the musty earth prepares for new life that will spring forth. As we examine the landscape, not long ago covered in a blanket of snow, we are aroused by the delicate protrusions breaking forth from the earth, pushing leaves aside. Quickly, and almost overnight, flowers bloom and decorate the environment with new color and fragrance. The trees put forth buds in preparation for leaves unfurling to become the shade of the new year.

The birds celebrate with song and begin their diligent search for that perfect spot to begin building new nests so that new life can be brought forth. The bee's start to appear, gorging themselves on the sweet nectar of the first spring flowers, whose aroma saturates the air and infuses the nostrils. While nearing a swampy area you are startled by the season's first cacophonous peeping of the chorus frogs, that builds with crescendo, but abruptly ends, almost as if they know you have arrived. Oh that first sound of the peepers tell that spring has arrived.

Although the tree squirrels in our area don't actually hibernate during the winter months, they limit their activities to consume energy. After a winter nestled in their tree nests, known as dreys, snuggling with members of their family, they no longer need to cover themselves with a furry tail to stay warm. Neither do they have to search for those hidden stores of food. They become more active and rejoice by rushing from limb to limb as if the warmth of the new season has rejuvenated their spirit.

When you approach the edge of the woods your excitement grows as you observe the occasional blue carpet of delicate flowers called Blue-Eyed grass. The dark blue flowers hang almost upside down, as if shielding their small yellow center from the casual observer, and are always a sure sign that winter is gone.

Upon exploration of the rich areas of the woods you find that some spring flowers are plentiful but allusive. The Trout Lily, also known as the Yellow Adder's Tongue, with its delicate yellow nodding flower, almost disappears with its leaves mottled with brown and blending into its surroundings. Natures camouflage at its best.

The Dutchman's Breeches, a small enchanting white flower, with many hanging in a row the length of its stalk, appearing like pairs of pantaloons hanging out to dry. The Bloodroot, with its single white flower and a single leaf that surrounds, protects, and cradles the flower stem as it grows taller. As the flower dies off, the deep lobed leaf opens large and flat like a solar panel to collect the rays of the sun. Of course, as spring progresses, you must not miss the short lived Purple Trillium. A gorgeous maroon or dark purple flower with a single whorl of three leaves: hence its name trillium.

We await the delicate cone shaped morels, almost brain-like until you realize they are actually pitted ridges, unlike the false morel. They will come soon, but not soon enough. But, Spring has arrived in all its glory. The season of awakening is here. A revival for both earth and our being.

# Rhythm of The Rain

# Rhythm of The Rain

There are various elements associated with the rain which affects many of our senses. This sensory stimulus provides us with memories that can be revisited by merely closing our eyes and recalling them in our mind. The smells, feelings, sights, and sounds, all work in tandem to create these memories.

Oftentimes, even before it arrives, the nose senses the subtle alteration in the smell of a breeze that tells us the rain is on the way. As the rain arrives, and begins to fall, it brings with it a fragrance of freshness. And as it departs, it leaves that musty scent of dampness.

A strong windblown rain can almost sting as it pelts the skin with a tenacity that is unexpected from a mere droplet of water. You can feel the moisture upon your skin, whether merely misted, or drenched. That clammy feeling of standing in damp clothing in hopes that the sun will reappear and warm the chill that encroaches on your soul, especially present when the weather is windy and cold. Yet when the temperatures are hot, the wetness is a welcome friend that tends to reduce the effects of the heat through the process of evaporative cooling.

The visual aspects of rain also create memories. Rain drops bouncing off a hard surface, almost as if they were dancing, yet transforming from actual drops to mini splashes of moisture, yet both being liquid. We have all experienced the nearly solid wall of rain, often called a sheet of rain, almost obscuring your vision beyond, but remaining transparent enough to provide a blurred view of what exists on the other side. With a heavy wind, this wall of rain can appear as if it is traveling vertical, like the strong spray from a hose.

When the rain lands on water it presents a show all of its own. As the rain strikes the water, each drop creates a circular wave, These concentric rings of miniature waves move outward from their center, enlarging in size until they collide with the numerous rings around them. And who can forget the droplets of rain on a large leaf, impersonating a magnifying glass, revealing the spectacle beneath in larger proportions than they actually exist.

But the sounds of the rain are what I remember the most. It is the rhythm of the rain that provides these auditory memories. The methodical beat produced by a particular rain can forge a memory based on the audible pattern created. The resonance, flow, and tempo, are all part of the rhythmic movement that helps to create these lasting retrospections.

Sometimes the rain beats hard, like an excited heart. Yet other times it barely presents a melodic tone as it gently sprinkles upon the earth. A rain can start lightly, building in crescendo, until the ultimate resonance drowns out all peripheral sounds.

There are also those unmistakable sounds that become your favorite. The patter of rain against a windowpane or the distinct "dink" of rain on a metal roof or aluminum boat. The sound of tires against a wet road that tells you, even without looking, that the rain had come.

For myself, it is the tempo of a constant rain upon my tent. I can lay there and intently listen to the comforting sound as it relaxes my being and soothes my soul until I pass from consciousness to slumber. It is this transition, caused by the rhythm of the rain, that I fondly recall.

# Butterflies

# Butterflies

Butterflies are delicate, majestic, and like anything of beauty, arouse your attention, consideration, and appreciation. I can spend hours watching butterflies as they lite upon the vivid array of flowers available in our yard. Of course, the flowers spikes of our butterfly bush is an irresistible lure , and they gather there by the dozens. But the cone flower, also known as Echinacea purpurea, is an obvious close second-place as a favorite attraction. Their primary food source is the nectar of these flowers, and we try to provide them with a smorgasbord to choose from.

These airborne beauties start life as a caterpillar and evolve into a fluttering attraction for all to watch and enjoy. Unfortunately, many of these beautiful creatures only live two to four weeks. But, those who migrate, like the monarchs, fly great distance to grace us with their presence and live as long as nine months.

Butterflies use a pair of antennae to sense the air for wind and scents, which assist them in locating the sweet nectar they desire. They also have compound eyes, providing them a well developed vision, that is most sensitive to the ultraviolet spectrum. Like bees, the ability to see in this spectrum provides them with a unique view that we, as humans, cannot appreciate. We look at a flower and see the beauty of the color and texture. A butterfly sees a pattern, almost like arrows on a landing strip, that leads them directly to the source of pollen and nectar.

The fluttering flight of the butterfly appears almost mechanical in nature. It often appears jerky, spasmodic, and almost labored, yet dignified in its own right You have to see a butterfly to know it is near. Pressing against the air under its wings, flight is as silent as the sound of one hand clapping.

Flight is conducted with two pairs of large wings, which are covered with thousands of tiny, overlapping, iridescent scales, that cover a transparent substance called chitin. The chitin becomes like a painter's canvass, and the scales reflecting light, like a painter's palette. The combination radiates a spectrum of colors, like a stained glass window, which provides the vivid and impressive patterns that we behold.

Upon locating the host for the nectar it seeks, it steadies itself on six jointed legs. It then sips on the nectar through a straw-like tube called a proboscis. Unlike the nervousness of the hummingbird, they look relaxed and content, like sitting on a veranda sipping an afternoon cocktail. When the meal is complete, the proboscis rolls up into a compact ball, and it is off to the next meal.

Butterflies are a summer treat and adornment that never cease to peak our interest or entertain. They are magical, and a lovely and pleasurable element of the season. They are missed when they are gone, and the waiting begins for their return the following year.

# Tree Moss

# Tree Moss

I have always had an affinity for tree moss. Emerald green in color, tree moss grows around the base of live trees and on fallen trunks, and give a mystical appearance to the woods. The eeriness of the shaded environment in which they grow, is overcome by its alluring beauty, like a layer of green felt, providing a soft and cushiony facade.

Moss does not happen upon this setting or habitat by chance. It is not an unintentional occurrence created by the spirit of the forest. The gloomy dimness of the surroundings in which the moss exists and flourishes is a result of its needs, not a supernatural inducement.

Moss grows in damp, shady locations because they are non-vascular plants, known as bryophytes. They lack vascular tissue, therefore they cannot retain water, nor have the ability to deliver it to other parts of their plant body. Since they have no way of transporting water through the plant, they must have a damp environment to grow, and reproduce. Reproduction is accomplished using spores, not seeds, and so they do not have flowers.

Even though moss likes the shade, they are autotrophic, and require at least enough sunlight to conduct photosynthesis. They are capable of self-nourishment by using inorganic materials as a source of nutrients, but need sunlight as a source of energy.

Some people wonder if this charming moss will injure or endanger the tree on which it covers like a delicate and supple blanket of green. But, not to worry. Being a epiphyte, moss is a plant that grows non-parasitically upon another plant. Its moisture and nutrients are acquired from the air, rain, and even from the accumulated debris around the tree's base, but not from the tree to which it is attached. But you ask, how can this be? Well, moss does not have any roots. They are anchored by threadlike rhizoids, which are simply hair-like protuberances that extend from the lower epidermal cells of bryophytes.

But even without knowing the technical details, when we find and observe this elegant and fascination adornment of the woods, it entices us, and beckons us to stare at its docile yet seductive beautifulness. You often can't resist touching its softness. Like a sponge, it absorbs your touch, and the impression you leave in its substance, slowly rises and returns to its original form.

It's form is luxurious, and blankets its host like the well manicured green of a golf course. A phenomenon of nature that provides us with a serene and lasting image of the inner being of the woods. An enduring impression that lives, even in our mind's eye. Existing in solitude and peace, the tree moss is an affecting entity.

# The Pond

# The Pond

When you were young, there was always that special place that you went to be alone, to contemplate what little you knew about life; a place of seclusion where you felt secure. Those places varied for each of us, depending on our location, natural surroundings, specific environment, and of course, our own particular and peculiar needs. A unique place that would accommodate the appropriate and distinct requirements of one, but not necessarily those of another. The place had to be in harmony with who and what you were, or at least wanted to be.

For me, that place was a small secluded pond about a quarter mile into the woods across from my home. The woods were dense and didn't start to become sparse until you came to that small body of water that appeared as though it had been magically situated for the sole purpose of providing me with a place of solitude.

At one end of the pond a small knoll rose gently up, and away from the pond to a height of maybe ten feet above the surrounding terrain. The entire knoll was only about twenty feet wide by thirty feet in depth, but it had small rock outcrops on each side and the rear. From the pond it appeared as a natural and mysterious throne,  having been created to rule the life at its feet.  But from the knoll, it became a sanctuary, with protection from all but the pond side.  Once the discovery was made, it became my place, and remained so for years.

In one aspect, it was a place to recline and allow the mind to ponder those things that yet made sense. In another, it was a place unrestricted by the shackles of adult intervention.  This was the time in life when the restrictions of a parent were necessary for your well being, but fought as a means to become who you were; who you wanted to be.

The pond was a place to explore and discover nature, and it was omnipresent.  There was a diverse selection of both flora and fauna and, in seclusion, they appeared more vivid and alive than a mere quarter mile away.  The sights and sounds took on a new meaning.  Time would seem to evaporate as the uninterrupted observation of a squirrel cracking open a nut, its cheeks being filled with the bounty at hand, made you wonder if any was being enjoyed now, or would only be saved for later.  Waiting for a frog, floating below the water's surface with eyes appearing to be fixed directly on you, to move, speculating if it was real and alive.

Through the seasons you could watch new plants welcomed into the world, and then progress through the various stages of growth and existence, learning much about both them, and yourself. As they developed, so did you, in both thoughts and perceptions. You came to realize that even those things that seemed trivial, or provided a spectacular beauty, remained on earth but a short time. The reasoning for their being was not always comprehended, but you came to realize, that there was a purpose.

And so you continued to enjoy the serenity of your special place. You continued to explore both the outer world and the inner being that was not what you were, but what you would be. Although the youthful visions of your future were sure to change, the memories of that special place remains. A place that, for the first time, you were allowed to examine and envision things that were unencumbered by the restraints, mandates, or persuasions of those who loved you, but didn't understand your needs to develop your individuality.

My place was the pond and much of what I am was initiated and developed there. Even though it has been many years, the place remains special in my recollections and remembrance of those days when my life was still ahead of me and my vision for the future had yet to be realized.

# The New Trail

# The New Trail

The pleasure of hiking a new trail is like reading a new book. Each turn of the trail is like the turn of a page. You never know what will come next, but you continue with unbridled anticipation.

Each new scene is for the first time, yet impatience often leads the mind to conjecture what lies ahead before the actual scene is revealed. Often the predictions are fallacious but the result can be pleasure or disappointment.

But you push forth with both your mind and your senses. You examine the all encompassing surroundings both close and at a distance. You hear the rustle of leaves with your aural senses and the magic of vision allows you to focus in on the scampering squirrel that caused the rustle and triggered the reaction to your senses. A stream is ahead... you know this because you can hear it before it comes into view.

The smells of the trail are new as well. The mustiness of a moist decaying forest floor disturbed by your steps or the breeze at a ridge that reminds you of another time and place. The seasonal smells of Spring, Summer, Fall, and Winter. All distinct on their own, but when blended and infused with the scent of the trail, help create a future reminiscence of this particular trail.

Often a trail will lead you through various environments. You might start through a forest with the morning mist dancing just above the floor and later trudge through a marshy area with swarms of mosquitoes and the croaks of frogs. As you lean into an uphill section a breezes frees you of the biting menace and evaporates the perspiration providing a coolness to your skin. A ridge provides scenes that were hidden in the dense canopy below and reveals the spectacle of the trail yet to come. The warmth of the sun motivates you to trek towards that newly discovered section of trail.

You unintentionally kick an acorn which necessitates an upward glance to confirm what you already know; an oak tree is somewhere above. You observe a large burl on the side of a tree and wonder what size bowl it would make if sliced off and carved. You observe moss on the side of a tree and wonder if it is the north side, knowing that moss actually grows on all sides of tree. Although the day is warm, a sudden drop in ambient temperature reveals you have entered a microclimate, and the coolness feels good. But just as quickly the temperature returns to normal and you know you have passed through this phenomenon of nature.

As you round a corner you stop abruptly. A doe and her fawn, with its camouflaging spots to hide in the underbrush, stand alongside the trail ahead. They don't run, but they know you are there. The fawn continues to nibble as the mother watches you with mistrust. As you remain stationary the standoff continues, until the doe cautiously crosses the trail, never taking an eye off your position. She disappears over a slight ridge, with the fawn in tow. Your hike can now continue.

The turns and discoveries continue until suddenly, as you round a corner, the trail ends and your time here is over. You leave the trail as you would close a book... sometimes satisfied, yet sometimes not. But either way, a day on a new trail is better than a day at work.

# Ruby-Throated Hummingbirds

# Ruby-Throated Hummingbirds

I have always had an affinity for the dainty and delicate hummingbird, a precious jewel of the bird kingdom. They are one of smallest of the bird species, yet in my opinion, one of the most amusing and interesting to attentively observe. I reside in the northeastern United States and it is the Ruby-Throated Hummingbird that is indigenous to my area. Although they migrate south to Mexico and South America to spend their winters, I patiently await their return, around May, so that I can once again begin to observe them; one of my favorite summer pastimes.

The Ruby-Throated Humming bird is miniature in size and measures only about three and a half inches long from the top of its head to the end of its tail. But the actual body is only about the size of an average thumb, and, overall, weigh less than a penny. Although they are dull colored on the bottom, the feathers provide their real beauty. The resplendent colors in iridescent hues of green sparkles like the ripples of water in the sun. Yet it is only the male that has the bright red throat, and a forked tail. The females were not adorned with the ruby throat and were relegated to a blunt tail with white tips.

The hummingbird got its name, not because it hums, but because of the humming or buzzing sound it makes when in flight. I am normally alerted to their presence by this sound, which reminds one of a large bee in flight, but, at least to me, is discernible and unique to the hummingbird. Bestowed with incredible speed, it is my understanding that they can reach speeds of twenty-five to thirty-five miles per hour and have been known to reach up to fifty miles per hour when diving. Rather amazing for such a small creature.

Although its needle like bill is long and straight, and appears like a hypodermic syringe for nectar, it does not function like that of the probe of a mosquito that actually sucks blood from its victim. The hummingbird's bill is inserted into the nectar area, then opened only far enough so that the tongue can do the work of obtaining the nectar.

Hummingbirds are attracted to flowers in shades of red, orange, and bright pink, but I believe they prefer bright red. I watch them intensely as they feed on my Cardinal Flowers and Bee Balm, both having flowers bright red in color, and apparently very delectable to their palate. From flower, to flower, to flower, they move in a spurt and then remain stationary in mid-air, being held in place only by the miniature wings flapping at an incredible speed. After obtaining the nectar they desire, and require, they perform a quick flight to the rear, and are the only bird that can do so. They again remain stationary in mid-air, almost as if inspecting the flower from which they feed, then off to the next. Finally, full of the sweet nourishment, they shoot off, like a bullet from a gun, to their place of solitude.

As a prelude to feeding, I often observe them perched on a petite branch concealed amongst the leaves of a tree, selecting the same branch every time. Except for an infrequent movement, they sit almost immobile, as if frozen in time, saving their energy for the next round of feeding. Finally, the decision is made and a beeline to the flowers containing the sweet nectar is sudden and swift and the feeding frenzy begins again.

Hummingbirds are anti-social and live a life of chosen solitude. Being they never fly or migrate together, a flock of hummingbirds will never be observed. Like a hermit of the forest, a hummingbird is a recluse who prefers a secluded and solitary life. Other than mating, they remain, like a spinster, unaccompanied.

These little birds are intensely aggressive and emphatically territorial. I have observed them chase each other at high speed, diving and evading, yet rarely a physical confrontation. Although a rare slam to the body will occur, the chase is the rule and usually results in the dominant retaining its territory while the defeated relinquishes and retreats to a location unknown.

I often sit in my screened in porch at the rear of my home and am always surprised when I hear one of these miniature summer comrades. Often I turn to observe them immobile in mid-air, staring at me through the screen, as if to say "Hello." They truly seem to recognize me as a friend. And yet, as autumn approaches, I know they must migrate south, to their winter domicile. But I know, like all good friends, they will eventually return and I will enjoy their company again.

# Weeds Can Feed

# Weeds Can Feed

When we have guests over for dinner, we usually like to start the meal with a salad. When the salad is placed on the table, and after a bewildered examination by our guests, we are normally informed that the salad looks splendid, but then asked what is in it.

Our salads seldom resemble the usual mixture of lettuces and greens presented at your normal table and are often full of color. Yet the contents are rarely identifiable by the ordinary diner. I usually retort that the contents are merely weeds and that the main course will probably contain more. Although surprised at the outset, before the salad is completed, compliments range from delicious to an epicurean's delight.

Most people just don't realize the plethora of weeds around their yard that are edible, healthy, and delectable. Weeds are often pulled up around the yard and garden as a nuisance without realizing they can be as healthy and delicious as the vegetables grown in the garden. And best of all, weeds are free for the taking. So let's examine some of those weeds that can feed in the Northeast where we reside.

In the early spring, you have the young Dandelion greens. The leaves of the dandelion are so toothed that it got its name from the French which means "lions tooth." Dandelions are well known, and usually dreaded, as the yellow fuzzy headed plant that tends to take over your lawn. But in the early spring, before they form those pinnacles of yellow flowers, and are still in the small rosette of leaves stage, they are not yet too bitter to eat. At this time, the small leaves, especially the pale whitish portion just below the soil, can be a great addition to salads, adding a little olive oil, lemon juice, and a pinch of salt. As a potherb, these young leaves can also be boiled or steamed for five to ten minutes. Either way, they are full of vitamins A and C. However, they do cook down, so collect plenty if you are using them as a potherb.

As the season progresses, and the flowers appear, dandelions become too bitter to eat. However, you can still use the yellow flower heads by dipping them in batter and deep frying them, like a fritter. As a last resort, you can bake the roots until brown and then grind them for use as you would any commercial coffee. Although a little bitter, it can be used as a coffee extender in an emergency situation, by mixing it with your commercial blend.

The Common Blue Violet is a spring flower which, at least on our property, seems to flower everywhere. Blue to violet in color, this delicate and charming flower has five petals with the lowest petal being longer and heavily veined. The side petals are bearded with long, thin, hairs on the inside portion, and the leaves are heart shaped. Although somewhat bland in taste, both the leaves and flowers add a nice touch to a completed salad, with the flowers contributing a pleasing dash of color. They are also rich in both vitamins A and C.

The Common Chickweed is another prolific plant that appears everywhere and can be eaten all year long. If you remember where it is grows, you can even find it growing under the snow in the winter, and harvest it for consumption. A small plant, normally laying flat on the ground, it has a flower so small it normally goes unnoticed. Yet, if one was to examine it closely they would discern that the miniature flower is notched so deeply that it appears to have ten petals as opposed to its actual five. With slender stems, the leaves grow in pairs. Common chickweed makes a pleasant addition to a salad, and we often have a salad with just chickweed and violets. They can be boiled or steamed for about five minutes as well, for use as a potherb.

An often overlooked weed is Purslane, which to the chagrin of many, grows well in every garden and many other areas around the yard. It is a smooth prostrate plant with reddish-green stems, with small paddle-shaped leaves. It has leaves and stems that have a sweet-sour flavor and are mucilaginous. They are another weed that is rich in vitamins A and C, with the addition of calcium and phosphorus. They make a great addition to a salad raw, and can be cooked and pickled as well. You can also use the seeds to make a nutritious flour.

Once salad is completed, there is an abundance of other weeds that just keep filling our pots with steamed or boiled greens. In the spring, we can't wait for the Ostrich Fern Fiddleheads. Still all curled up at the heads, like a kitten against its mother, they are great steamed. And don't forget to leave some of the stems attached, as they are as tasty as the fiddleheads. Unfortunately, once they uncurl, they become poisonous, so enjoy them when you can.

One of my favorites all summer and early fall, which I rarely hear about, is the Asiatic Dayflower. Often ignored, this delicate little beauty is my preferred steamed potherb. It is a dainty little blue flower that has two large petals above, that stick out like mouse ears. It has one diminutive white petal below that hangs like a an old man's beard. The flower has three long white stamens below that appear like bean sprouts, but the upper three are shorter and look like miniature yellow and burgundy flowers. It has lance shaped leaves, and it is those leaves that you collect and cook. We are fortunate to have a plenitude of these graceful and attractive flowers in various areas of our property where it is shady or moist.

The Stinging Nettle is another excellent pot herb. Nettles have little stinging hairs on the stems and the leaves, so use caution when harvesting them. Gloves are recommended, and either keep your arms and wrists covered, or avoid having the plant rub on either. The Stinging Nettle has leaves that are coarsely toothed and are in opposite pairs every few inches on the upper portion of the stalk. The leaves are ovate to lanceolate in shape and usually have a heart-shaped base. Small greenish flowers appear in small, branching clusters, from the leaf axils. In the spring you can pick the upper two or three pairs of leaves, but by summer I recommend only the upper two. As a steamed or boiled potherb, it doesn't get much better than Stinging Nettle, and as soon as they are cooked, the stinging properties disappear.

Galinsoga is a weed that constantly tries to take over our vegetable garden, and is rarely discussed when edible weeds are mentioned. A low inconspicuous weed with slender forking stems, the leaves are broad, opposite, and coarsely-toothed. The miniature little flowers are only about one-quarter inch across with five tiny three lobed rays around a golden central disc. Again, it is the leaves that are eaten as a cooked green. Steamed or boiled, they are great served with butter. As with most potherbs, they really cook down, so again you should pick plenty.

Lamb's Quarters is also known as Goosefoot because the leaves remind some of a goose's foot. It is both, a weed that can be used raw in salads, or cooked as a potherb, and they are delicious both ways. The leaves, which get up to four inches long, are somewhat diamond shaped when mature and broadly toothed. They grow alternately from the stalk on petioles about half the length of the leaf. Although they are a dark bluish-green color on the top, the underside is usually covered with a whitish-gray powder. The small, upper most leaves on mature plants have more of a lanceolate shape and lack teeth on their margins.

Closely related to spinach, Lamb's Quarters can be eaten from spring through fall. In the spring, until the plant reaches up to twelve inches, you can normally use the entire plant as a cooked potherb. The tender upper leaves are great as an addition to a salad. As the plant gets larger, select the upper more tender leaves for cooking. It should also be noted that the Lamb's Quarters' little black seeds, available in late fall, can be boiled and used to make a breakfast type gruel, or ground into flour. They are very nutritious.

Amaranth is another good weed, that seems to love my garden. It has a course stout stem that averages about three to four feet tall, but are known to get as high as six feet. The leaves are dull green and are ovate to lance shaped, with toothless borders, and grow alternatively on the stem. The tender leaves can be used in a salad and make a good potherb. In the late summer and fall, they develop flower clusters in the leaf axils that are dense. The seeds from these clusters can be used to make flour.

Lady's thumb is an acceptable potherb and the young leaves can also be used in a salad. It is an upright standing plant with tiny pink clusters of flowers and narrow leaves. It is unique in that each leaf has a dark triangular mark on it that resembles a thumb print, hence the name "Lady's Thumb."

If you are lucky enough to have Jerusalem Artichoke on your property, you are in for a treat. It can be considered a true survival food and one of the best! It is a member of the sunflower family and is also known as Sun choke. The leaves have a rough, hairy texture, that seem to drag along a bare arm, but do no harm. The larger leaves on the lower stem are opposite and can be up to 12 inches long. The higher leaves are smaller, narrower, and alternate. The flowers, like a sunflower, bestow a splendid hue of yellow, with a center that is brownish gold.

Although the flowers are attractive, it is the tubers underground that are edible. Some of these tubers, getting as large as a medium size potato, can be eaten raw by slicing them thin and adding them to a salad. The tubers can be substituted in recipes that call for potatoes. Locate them while they are still flowering, then dig up the tubers throughout the fall, and even the winter if the ground becomes unfrozen. Although the consumption of the tubers have been known to cause flatulence, I find that prudent consumption reduces the consequence.

All of the plants discussed here grow wild around our property and they often provide almost as much feasting as our garden. For those used as potherbs, like spinach, they all cook down so pick a lot. As you can see, weeds are everywhere, but not all are bad. They can be a healthy addition to any meal and are free for the taking. As a warning, you should never pick and eat a plant that you have not one hundred percent identified as edible As you learn the proper identification of your local edible plants, you will find that, weeds can feed!

# I Made Fire!

# I Made Fire!

In an emergency situation in the wilderness, there is a commodity that can be the difference between surviving and expiring. A remarkable array of resources are made available by a magical combination of oxygen, heat, and fuel. This extraordinary combination provides the ultimate survival asset - fire!

Most people realize that fire can produce heat. That warmth that permeates the soul when a deep chill has just about convinced you that you will never again feel warm. But there is so much more. Fire provides light which allows you to see when darkness comes. It allows you to dry your clothes when wet from either rain or submersion in water. It provides a means of signaling, whereby an abundance of billowing white or black smoke (whichever one contrasts best against your background) could identify your position to those looking for you. The use of fire can boil water in order to purify it for safe drinking and use. Fire can be used to cook in order to, either make food safe to eat, or make it more palatable. Fire can make tools and useful devices such as spoons, bowls, and even fire hardened spears.

One of the often overlooked benefits of fire is a sense of companionship. A friend in the dark that helps repel the noises of the night. Fire provides comfort and is a morale builder. You are not alone because you have your friend, your fire. The warmth and light it provides dispenses comfort, renews your spirit, and revives self-confidence.

This is why those persons in the know - those who practice their survival skills before they need them, become elated when they make fire. Just watch a person using the bow and drill technique in an attempt to make fire. After fashioning and assembling the required components, an intensity of conviction consumes their motion. The methodical spinning of the spindle, with a makeshift bow, continues until the initial wisps of smoke erupts from the fireboard. The spinning of the spindle is then magnified and pressure on the spindle intensifies. As the smoke changes in color, a different smell exudes from the fire board, and the spinning stops. The spindle is held on top of the fire board momentarily to contain the heat. Finally, as the spindle is cautiously lifted, an ember appears.

The ember is gently transferred to a tinder bundle that has been carefully and meticulously molded and fabricated for the purpose of turning the sacred ember into flame. The tinder bundle is held high, cradling the ember inside, to prevent the eventual smoke from blinding your actions. The initial blowing into the bundle is slow and easy. White smokes erupts, lightly at first, but as the blowing of the ember intensifies, so does the smoke.

Then suddenly, it appears. Like magic, flames erupt from the tinder bundle, and it appears as if a miracle has occurred. Fire has been created by the hand of man and the person almost always, at least the first time, exclaims, "I Made Fire." The importance of what they have created is only subtly comprehended.

# The Woods Have No Keepers

# The Woods Have No Keepers

The woods are pristine in their own way. Although self occurring debris litters the woods, it is internal, and integral, to the natural process of self maintenance. A dead tree may fall and rot, but returns its nourishment to the forest floor, to nurture future growth. This is natural and does not look out of place. It belongs there and we expect it.

However, when you enter the forest with an anticipated glimpse of uncorrupted nature, and you view the litter of humans, it ruins the naturalness of the woods. Water bottles, jerky wrappers, cigarette butts, tissue, etc. It disrupts the natural aura of the woods and reminds you that many humans "don't get it."

The woods can maintain its own balance from those natural occurring, and internal, litter that is self producing. But it does not have the means to cleanse itself of non-natural waste. I can only think of two types of people who would be so thoughtless or careless as to leave man made debris in the woods.

The first that comes to mind are those, that like children, have always had someone picking up after them. A mommy, a wife, a servant, or other type person who's purpose is to walk around behind that person, and clean the mess they cause. These type of people need to learn self maintenance and to be responsible for their own litter. Most of these people, although no longer children, are probably destined to continue in their path of ignorance of what goes on around them, and how their actions affect others.

The second type of person just doesn't care. Even though they are aware of their actions, such as they carried it in, they just don't believe it is their responsibility, to carry it out. They are "special" and the rest of the world is here to support their "specialness." These are the same type of people who think they don't have to abide by the rules that are for "other people." These are the people who park in a handicap spot when they don't have a handicap, because the space is closer to the door, and after all, they are "special." These individuals are usually a lost cause. They are "special" and the woods are there for them to enjoy, and if they litter... Oh well, not their concern.

The woods are special to me. I always endeavor to leave them in pristine condition, so that the next person down the trail gets to enjoy the same beauty as I. I am not there to cleanse the woods of debris left by those who either don't understand, or don't care... But I do.

Therefore, I ask that if you fit one of the two descriptions above, would you please do me a "special" favor?   Stay Out Of The Woods and Off the Trails. The Woods Have No Keepers.

# Nature's Double-Edged Sword

# Nature's Double-Edged Sword

When in the outdoors, Mother Nature can be our provider and furnish many of the essentials we need to survive. However, she can be a powerful force to reckon with. All the positive things that she offers can also be turned against us. She can be a double edged sword.

She can provide the much needed water from her streams, creeks and ponds. The rain from the skies can moisten our lips and be accumulated in containers for future hydration. But sudden immersion, or violent currents, can also lead to sudden death. The rain that provides needed hydration can also inundate an inappropriately located shelter, or wash it away with a flash flood.

The materials required for a shelter are all there in nature. Shelter can be offered from a downed tree, with insulation from the cold procured from the fallen leaves which have accumulated on the ground, or the boughs of a coniferous tree. A cave or rock overhang can provide instant refuge from a sudden downpour. You need only be able to recognize what is offered and utilize that serviceability. But choose your site carefully as a falling dead tree, branch, or old stream bed suddenly raging with water, can transform your comfort into chaos.

Fire is an important element of survival and the essentials for the making a fire are available in nature as well. The materials only need to be perceived by the discriminate eye, and a possession of the skills needed to utilize that which is found for the purpose of producing a fire. However, this important commodity, used to warm our being, must be attended with mindful and cautious vigilance. Fire, both friend and foe, if allowed to get out of hand, can result in a conflagration destroying that same being it protects.

The weather can change quickly, transforming a refreshing breeze into heavy damaging winds, often producing catastrophic effects and consequences, especially from a forest's canopy. Lightning, although a dazzling attraction from afar, can become a deadly enemy when in its path of electrical energy.

Nature can provide food as well. Although, often unrecognized by the untrained eye, there are a plethora of edible plants available to the those who have studied their identification and preparation. But care must be taken as nature does not identify those that are, and are not, edible. Some plants that appear edible, if misidentified, can terminate a life without lament.

Meat and fish can often be procured to provide the essential proteins required for the continued efforts expended in an attempt to provide for one's self. This nourishment, thus energy, can be provided by nature as well. But, use caution and stay wary. The prey you seek, pursued for sustenance, can easily become the predator, and you become the meal.

If you want to survive in the wilderness, you must live within the bounds of Mother Nature's rules. You must attempt to live in harmony with nature. Like the tall trees in the wind, don't resist nature, but learn to bend with her. By adapting to what nature offers, and living within her bounds, you increase your chances of survival. Those who resist her power, perish!

# The House Wren

# The House Wren

I have always enjoyed watching the birds with their various mannerisms, attitudes, demeanor and personality. Some are more beautiful than others in color and song, but each have their own attributes and are no less interesting.

One of my favorite, and one of the most familiar backyard birds, is the House Wren. Diminutive in size, and dull in appearance, they make up for their smallness and nondescript features with an effervescent voice.. They have become our friends and an adjunct addition to our family. These little birds always present a calm disposition, and are diligent in their efforts to build a nest, and then tend to their young.

I often spend hours both watching and listening to the male House Wren as he sings his song to attract a mate. This can goes on for days, and even weeks, without ever showing signs of frustration or resignation. The song is delightful, fascinating, and alluring, as it charms the female to come inspect the potential nest. This may repeatedly result in the potential mate rejecting the location for reasons unknown, but the motivation of the male continues with the short burst of lively song.

Although the song starts with a few almost stuttering staccato notes, it quickly smoothes out and gains in rhythm and cadence, then ends abruptly. This continues throughout the day, and to my ears at least, it often sounds like the making of small stitches with a sewing machine: Short and careful at first, then a brief burst, and the stitch is made. The ballad is always the same, and is sung continuously until his mission of finding a mate is accomplished.

Once a mate accepts the nesting location, both the male and female work at making a nest that will cradle their newly born. Although the female lacks a song, once mating has occurred, she uses high-pitched squeals to communicate with the male. As the building begins, you can watch them hopping through the shrubs and ground-height branches, collecting building materials and snatching at insects. They are diligent in effort and purpose and the undertaking is accomplished in short order.

During this stage, you await the birth of the new family with anticipation. When birth occurs, the continuous feeding by both parents is a never ending activity. The babies grow up fast and soon you will see small open beaks protruding from the entrance hole beckoning to be feed. The parents fulfill the little insatiable appetites with relentless trips and boundless energy.

It is at this time that the friendly and bubbly chatter of song can become a scolding declaration and warning. This places you on notice that, even though we accept your presence, you must stay back and keep your distance. This is a distinct sound and much different than the song. Almost a small and muted crow call, you have no doubt you are being told you are too close and should back away.

Because I enjoy their company, I continue to build small bird houses specifically for the House Wren. I have spent hours constructing these individually unique houses, and none are the same. They are all about four inches by four inches square and four inches to six inches tall, but the finishing touches make each one different. The important aspect of these little structures are an entrance hole no more than one and one-eighth inches around, placed about six inches above the floor. The size of the hole ensures that other birds do not gain entrance to a house made specifically for our friends. I paint them in various pastel colors such as light yellow, lavender, and pink, accented with white. I have no evidence to prove that these colors attract these small songbirds, but none of the houses we build ever go uninhabited.

Never underestimate the pleasure that can be gained from a simple undertaking. The effort to provide a community for our little friends is repaid in the enjoyment of their presence. The little wren houses are all within view of our screened in porch and the sights and sounds enliven our existence and furnish never-ending entertainment for the summer months. They are members of our community and considered a part of our family.

# Wild Flowers

# Wild Flowers

Whether in a yard, a field, deep in the woods, on a mountainside, or along a stream, wild flowers are a thing of beauty unsurpassed by most other amenities.  Although the garden variety of flowers can also be exquisite, they are usually nurtured and pampered, whereby those in the wild must fight for their existence and survival in order to bring forth such radiant beauty.

Wild flowers decorate and embellish the environment in which they inhabit, and like the sun shining through a stained glass window, they can give new meaning to an otherwise somber setting.  Even in a habitat that might be naturally dismal, a delicate flower, vivid in color, can decorate the surroundings and enrich the lackluster.  A whole meadow of flowers can appear as a radiant carpet beckoning you to stroll through its majestic pathway of pleasure.

Have you ever wondered why flowers were bestowed with such beauty.  Although their pulchritude provides us with a plethora of colorful and fragrant images and enjoyment, the intention was not for the purpose of human pleasure, but to survive. Because there is a limited number of insects that pollinate flowers, over time and through evolution, they evolved into more beautiful and scented creations in order to attract insects for pollination. Much of this actually occurs in the ultraviolet spectrum which unfortunately is outside of the visible spectrum for humans. They are also colorful so that they stand out from the background, like a male Cardinal perched on the outer limb of a blue spruce.. Appearance, shape, and scent, are all for the purpose of attracting pollinators.

But for us, the human species, it is the visual splendor and fragrance, that attracts us. They adorn our environment like an ornament on a Christmas tree. They can beautify the dreary, reinvigorate the melancholy, and warm our heart. The visual delight and pleasurable redolence provides a temporary escape from reality and a replenishment of contentment. The discovery of a lustrous sample of the flower kingdom in the wilds can be as exciting as finding gold in a stream or a crystal protruding from the underside of a piece of quartz. The euphoria of that sudden find can be magical.

I always enjoy the sudden encounter with a wild flower when least expected. I recall the excitement and exhilaration upon rounding a rock ledge while hiking in the Alps with my wife. We had just dropped below the snow line and there on a south facing ledge were an exquisite array of majestic little flowers. The Spring Gentian, Alpine Snowbell, Stemless Gentian, and Purple Saxifrage. An impressive display of beauty, none of which I had ever seen before. Just observing them seemed to extract the chill from our being and brought warmth to our soul.

In the shaded woods, just coming upon the delicate Dutchmen's Breeches, appearing like pairs of pantaloons hung up to dry, can reinvigorate your journey. Or the sudden discovery of the Canada Mayflower, also known as Wild Lily-Of-The-Valley, reveals how such a small woodland plant can brighten your day.

Once while exploring a swampy area, I came upon the Canada Lily. Unlike the Day Lily, it is more yellow and the flower droops downward as though nodding, with the petals and sepals curling backward. It was an elegant find when least expected. While hiking through a meadow that appeared all green while ascending a slope, as I reached the crest, it became a blanket of white, as the delicate Yarrow appeared all around me. You just never know when that next wild flower will enter your life and change your mood.

Although we are not pollinators, we are appreciators, of the wild flower. The shapes, the colors, the fragrances, all combine to draw us near. Wild flowers are magical and make our world a better place. They continue in their evolution to entice and beckon the pollinators who assist in their continued existence, but the result is the enlightenment of our environment and spirit.

# Needs Vs. Wants

# Needs Vs. Wants

One of the places I enjoy hiking on occasion is at the Vanderbilt Mansion National Historic Site, in Hyde Park, New York. It has a trail through the woods which runs parallel to the Hudson River and it provides splendid views of both the woods, and the river.

Next to the parking area, where the hike begins, a huge mansion sits upon a knoll overlooking the river. It is from an age of opulence and is lavishly adorned with marble and furnishings from France, in a most extravagant manner. The fascinating aspect of the mansion is that it was only considered a summer cottage for the Vanderbilt family, and used only a month or two out of the year, although a staff was maintained year round.

It has always confounded me as why anyone would need such ostentatious embellishments in order to revel in one's accomplishments. It would seem that often affluence begets improvident behavior.

I believe I have done fairly well in life, at least meeting my own expectations, but I've never endeavored to encompass myself with superfluous trappings denoting success. These artificial manifestations of attainment always seem to be nothing more than either, an ego gone awry, or a pretense for false prosperity. Fancy cars meant to impress, a residence that provides for more that my needs, or any other array of accouterments signifying wealth, have never been on my agenda.

I have always been a practical man, or at least I have tried to be. However, it seems unfortunate that many people get caught in this web of deceit and spend their lives trying to impress those, who in reality, mean little to ones existence. Everyone has heard of the old adage, "Keeping up with the Joneses," but few realize they are embarking on behavior that leads to the attainment of things for all the wrong reasons.

This behavior can also materialize in not only actions, but attitude. I once knew a couple who always threw their empty soda and beer cans and bottles in the garbage. I asked why they did that instead of recycling them. The husband informed me that he was a professional in the community, and then asked how it would look if someone saw him standing in front of a recycle machine pushing in old cans and bottles like some derelict. Apparently, his need to appear affluent was more important than the need to recycle.

My lifestyle has always been rather self-reliant. and I appreciate the ability to fend for myself. The tools and skills required to accomplish that endeavor has always outweighed the need to have those things, that might bring me pleasure, but at a cost of dependency on others that is counterproductive to my overall goals.

Of course, my goals are simplistic because my desire is to be as least dependent on others as reasonably possible. However, I understand that everyone's priorities are different than mine, and what is important to one person, might be insignificant to another. There are people who spend an exorbitant amount of time and money to keep their lawn beautiful, but don't have the time for a vegetable garden. They want a luxurious lawn, but don't have the need to provide for some of their own food. So they are dependent on weed killers, fertilizers, and other various lawn care products, and at the same time, they are dependent on the local market to obtain all of their food.

There are families in my area that have all of the adult toys such as motorcycles, all terrain vehicles, and snowmobiles. They have modern technology to include the most up-to-date cell phone, wide screen television, and satellite reception. One of these families live in an old trailer that always seems to be falling down around them, and another an old house in terrible disrepair. Both have a fairly large piece of land in the country, but neither of them have a vegetable garden. They don't seem to realize that their toys of enjoyment keep them forever dependent on others. We all need recreation, but I wonder at what cost. It would seem that these mechanisms of enjoyment just might adulterate their ability to succeed in a tangible manner.

Now don't get me wrong. It is not my place to judge other people or determine what makes one happy. I only look at life through my old eyes, and I find most things that I enjoy are free. Hiking, watching nature, growing beautiful plants and nourishing food, and a comfortable home, all provide me with inner satisfaction. I am also fortunate that I am without concern as to what other people think of me. Although toys can be fun, I decline to be shackled by those things that require my dependence on others, and in the long run, abridge my actual independence from others.

When you think about it, your actual needs are much less than most wants. If those needs were addressed, as opposed to the wants, you would gain the freedom of being less reliant on others to maintain a lifestyle that is only perceived as being important to others, or that only provides a false sense of enjoyment. Again, everyone has a right to those things in life that make them happy, and we all have different needs. But I have found, that often those things that we think will make us happy, only provide us with either further unhappiness, or more dependency on others. My desire is to live lightly on this earth, and that is a need of mine. My wants are always tempered by that need, and I can only hope that more people will realize that true enjoyment and satisfaction can come from less, not more.

# Autumn Is Upon Us

# Autumn Is Upon Us

Well, autumn is upon us again. I walk the trails and observe the vivid and iridescent medley of fall colors. The intensity of the red, orange, and yellow, produce a glowing brilliance from the sun's radiance against my skin. The fragrance of the early morning air is different upon my nostrils, cool and refreshing. The temperature is not yet frigid, but crisp enough to warrant that light wool sweater.

This time of year always takes my mind back to my youth. Memories of hayrides, apple cider, pumpkins, and corn husks. The coolness that would fade as the internal warmth elevated from the exertion of raking leaves. Making the piles, as high as the wind would permit. And then the jumping, and landing upon natures mattress, hearing the pleasant rustle and crinkle of the leaves under the weight of my being. The laughter of family and friends enjoying an autumn day.

As I continue on my jaunt, I notice some of the leaves are already brown, wrinkled, and fluttering to the ground. I can hear the rustle of the dried leaves beneath my feet as I walk. I recall as a child, being disheartened at the loss of leaves by the trees, like a parent losing a child. But my father, in his infinite wisdom, once explained that autumn was a time to rejoice. The leaves fall from their parental perch so they could collect at the trees feet. There, they would decay and nourish the soil, so that the parent could continue its natural cycle of producing new children. Next spring, new buds would reappear, bringing with them new leaves.

Well I'm a little older now, yet I recall my father's words. Autumn is a time to rejoice! As the scenery changes, the ground stiffens in preparation for winters cover. The leaves sleep so their natural decay nurtures future growth of the parent that brought them forth. Autumn is upon us, so don't be disheartened, but Rejoice!

# Hiking The Swiss Alps

# Hiking The Swiss Alps

If you have never had the pleasure of visiting the Swiss Alps, you have truly missed an experience of a lifetime!  Whenever I mention that I hiked the Swiss Alps, I'm often asked what precipitated such an excursion.  Well here is the story of how I got to hike the Swiss Alps.

I was brought up in New York and often hiked and camped in the Catskill and Adirondack mountains.  While I was dating my wife Denise, who is from Switzerland, I once tried to impress her by showing her the Adirondack High Peaks area.  Being the largest mountains I had ever seen personally, I knew she would be more than impressed.

After driving down through Keene, I asked what she thought.  Although she felt the area was beautiful, she lacked the excitement I thought she would exhibit. When I asked why she was not in awe of the height of the peaks, she asked, "Have you ever seen the Swiss Alps?"  I indicated that I had not, but that we had the Rocky Mountains here in the America, and it was my understanding they were rather formidable. She explained, that although she had been to the Rockies, and they were also beautiful, they lacked the intimacy of the views provided by the

Swiss Alp. She explained, that the Rockies started at about 1 mile above sea level, whereby you are already over 5,000 feet. With the largest peak being Mount Elbert, at 14,440 feet, you are only seeing about 9,000 feet of mountain face. The Alps start almost at sea level, so when you look at summits, you get the full effect of their height. She indicated that although the Matterhorn is 14,691 feet, there are over one hundred summits higher than 13,123 feet. Needless to say, I was sold.

The following year, I was on a plane to meet my future wife in Switzerland. After visiting her parents for the day, we headed out for a small town called Grindelwald. After driving extensive switchbacks, first going up and then back down, and traveling through extensive tunnel systems, we finally arrived after dark at the small town of Grindelwald. We headed to a small Swiss chalet which Denise had rented for a week. It had wonderful overhanging eves and an enchanting little balcony on which to view the surrounding countryside. I was excited, but only morning would satisfy my desire to see the Swiss Alps. I wondered how far we would have to travel to get a glimpse of these famous mountains, what made them so special, and were they really that big?

I woke up early, as I normally do, made a cup of coffee, and wandered out onto the balcony. I was immediately awe struck! My mind could not comprehend what was before my eyes. I yelled to Denise who strode out onto the balcony with a smile that concealed her inner feeling of delight in my reaction to the stunning splendor before me.

Immediately in front of me was the enormous surface of a mountain face that was so imposing I almost fell over backwards looking up at it. Seeing the quizzical look on my face, Denise simply retorted, "Oh, that is the North Face of Eiger". I said, "like the one in the movie "The Eiger Sanction" with Clint Eastwood?" She simply stated, "That would be the one".

As I looked around, I realized that Grindelwald was a small town that was situated as if it were in the bottom of a small cup. The sides of the cup surrounded the bottom as the Swiss Alps surrounded us. Denise started pointing, indicating that is Lauteraarhorn, Eiger, Mönch, Jungfrau, Männlichen, Rothorn, Grossenegg, Schwarzhorn, etc. There were many more, but I got the idea.

The colossal magnificence of the Swiss Alps is more than breathtaking. The height of the snow covered peaks are an imposing beauty that is difficult to comprehend visually as a reality. Mere photographs can never convey or reveal the magnitude or immensity of their size. A human can only feel insignificant in the presence of their splendor.

We started out that morning, grabbing our day packs, and taking a cable car that seemed to go up forever, in order to arrive at Männlichen, which brought us to 7,304 feet. From this point, we could observe the towering peaks all around us, like neighbors standing around together. First we enjoyed some coffee and croissants with black cherry jam at an eatery surrounded by huge glass windows which presented a panoramic view of the surrounding preeminence. It will go down as my most memorable breakfast.

We then headed for a hiking trail that wound around the edge of Tschuggen, from Männlichen to Kleine Scheidegg. From snow covered trails to open Alpine areas with delicate and exquisite flowers reaching toward the sun. Some areas of the trail had been covered by mini avalanches, but my guide, Denise, said not to worry. She had negotiated these type of trails many times before. The trail continued winding first up and then down, until we arrived at Kleine Scheidegg which was at 6,760 feet. It had been a long hike and I was able to rehydrate by partaking in a wonderful ale at an outdoor beer garden, know as a Biergarten.

The next day we took a cable car in the opposite direction as the previous day and arrived at

First, and took a trail up to Lake Bachalpsee, which is hidden behind Mount Röthorn, at 7,429 feet. It was a steep hike, and colder than the previous day. Looking at the trail map, we decided to hike down and vertical, across to Grosse Scheidegg, which took the rest of the day. A ride on a small bus down an extremely narrow switchback road was as memorable as the hike up.

Each day went this was. A new trail from a new angle allowed us to view the surrounding expanse of peaks from various perspectives. The sights I saw are indelibly etched in my mind. Many days I have closed my eyes and recall the splendor of the magnificent spectacle I will always know as the Swiss Alps. If you have never been there, it is a trip worthy of the time and expense.

# A Vegetable Garden

# A Vegetable Garden

It has been said that a garden is a labor of love. With a flower garden, you are compensated for your work with the beauty it provides. But a vegetable garden rewards your effort with delectable edibles. It bestows upon you nourishing sustenance that cannot be found fresher, anywhere. They can be consumed as they are picked, or preserved in various ways, to provide for your needs another day.

A vegetable garden starts even before spring arrives, if only in your mind. The planning of how it will be arranged this coming year, based on mistakes, if any, made the previous season, or to ensure crops are rotated to a new position. Seeds, which you gathered from last year's plants, or new ones purchased for those special varieties you want to try this coming year, must be started in small containers inside and nurtured into strong, healthy seedlings.

Finally, the smell is in the air, and you know spring is upon you. You head for your plot of soil that is better known as "The Garden." The earth, upon which your garden will be planted, must be worked. Using a garden fork, the soil is loosened and mounded into rows and sections, that have already been predetermined for specific plants. Often small stakes are inserted and string stretched between them to keep the rows neat and orderly. Seedlings are planted and row markers identify the occupants of those rows. Seeds are inserted and patted gently to welcome them to their new home. Tomato plants are carefully placed in the soil and wire cages set in place, in anticipation of their need to support the growth to come.

Your hands are soiled with the remnants of the earth in which you toiled. The aroma of the soil is upon them and it is a satisfying sensation. You have physically stirred the soil that will bring forth your bounty, and it is a gratifying feeling.

Next comes what I call the "3-Ws." This identifies the phase that requires weeding, watering, and waiting. The least favorable, yet the most important, aspect to ensure a healthy and plentiful crop come harvest time. Although the waiting begins, the labor does not end. The weeding continues throughout the growing season to ensure that your crops have the least amount of competition for the moisture in the soil. It is a combination of sunshine and water that brings forth your harvest, and it is a delicate balance. If your garden is too dry, growth will be slow and stunted. If it is too wet, your plants will rot in place.

Let's not forget the invasive insects that will destroy your crops if not properly managed, nor the four legged predators that will dine on your labor. Even when fenced, your garden will require constant vigilance for signs of those that wish to benefit from your hard work.

Finally, the vegetables mature and ripen. It is now time to harvest, eat, and preserve. The labor continues, but the fruit of all that labor has arrived. The freshness, taste, and nutrition of the vegetables you have grown, and begin to enjoy, cannot be equaled by any purchased at a store. The crops come forth faster than you can eat them, and the effort to preserve them is not something that can wait. The preservation process is hard work as well, but necessary in order to protect your bounty for the coming winter and spring.

This phase of your garden consists of cutting, hanging, and drying your herbs, which can then be stored in glass jars in a dark location. There is nothing better in the middle of the winter than some dried parsley or oregano for your tomato sauce, or a calming cup of mint tea.

Vegetables that are highly acidic, such as tomatoes, can be preserved using a boiling-water bath. This method will also be used for pickles, relishes, chutneys, all of which use vinegar, as well as most fruits and heavily sweetened jams and jellies.

Pressure canning will be required for those vegetables not preserved in vinegar, as they are low in acid, and the high temperature of this canning method will sterilize the food by destroying microorganisms such a botulism.

Of course, the use of a root cellar is a natural storage method that has been used since ancient times. In the early 1600's, the European colonists quickly adopted the Native American practice of storing food in underground pits in order to preserve it over the winter months. It is still a viable method today for storing crops such as potatoes, beets, carrots, onions, radishes, squash, and apples.

Whatever preservation method you choose, you will be extending the life of your harvest, ensuring home-grown food for the winter and through the following spring. It warms the heart and feeds the soul when your pantry provides an offering that came from your own harvest and hard work.

The final phase begins and the garden must be put to rest and the soil prepared for the following season. We cover our garden with leaves to blanket it for the winter, but a cover crop can be grown for the same purpose.

Yes, a vegetable garden is a labor of love, from beginning to end, but one that rewards you like no other. The labor is over, but it just might be time to start planning for next year's garden.

# A Pantry's Comfort

# A Pantry's Comfort

A pantry is almost a thing of the past. When I was a small boy in the fifties, having a supply of food at our home was as normal as a slingshot hanging out of a boys back pocket. Farmers harvested their crops then stored them for the winter to provide food through the spring. Root cellars and home canning was standard behavior. Unfortunately, this type of mindset today seems to be considered the activity of hoarders or those expecting an apocalypse.

As years have progressed since my childhood, and with the advent of a grocery store within close proximity of every neighborhood, the storing of extra food has become the exception, as opposed to the rule. Why bother when you can just stop at the local market for those needed provisions?

Other things have changed as well. Grocery stores used to have a warehouse behind the shopping area. Restocking of shelves could be accomplished without the need for daily deliveries by trucks. This has changed as well. Now, what you see is what they have, and when it's gone, well it's gone.

In the world in which we live, unforeseen occurrences can develop in the blink of an eye. One day we sit comfortably in our home, content and satisfied with the present course of life's direction. But lurking just around the corner, like a mugger in the night, natural and unnatural disasters wait. Natural disasters can disrupt the natural course of everyday life. All of a sudden, the shelves at the local grocery store, normally fully stocked as if by magic, are empty. The loss of income, through no fault of your own, could limit and restrict the typical contribution to provisions.

What a wonderful sense of comfort a pantry provides, knowing that if an emergency presents itself, the essentials for nourishment are at hand. Having lived most of my life in the country, I learned early on that when times are bad, food can be a great soother, appeaser, comforter, and motivator. When there are few things we can depend on, a pantry sets with sustenance, just waiting for the chance at rescue.

A pantry is your own little grocery store, with shelves stocked with all those foodstuffs, just waiting to be chosen to assist with the early morning refueling, midday nourishment, or the evening meal. The rows of cans, glass jars, sealed buckets, lined up like troops, waiting to liberate your hunger. Vegetables, legumes, staples like salt, sugar, flour, etc, are all there. A family of provisions just waiting to serve.

A pantry is like an insurance policy for both stomach and morale. A repository of hope. For both survival and self reliance, a pantry is a provident plan for peace of mind.

# Our Own Mortality

© JDM

# Our Own Mortality

I have a t-shirt that says, "My own mortality will be the death of me yet." Some people laugh when they see it, some don't understand it, and others put forth a quizzical expression. But the fact is, with life comes the comprehension that we will someday expire.

I can remember as a small child, the first time that I became aware of the fact that I would someday die. I recall that I couldn't fathom the reality, as my life was just beginning, and the actuality that I would eventually perish seemed abstract. Then what was the purpose of life? Why are you born to only die? Being young, like being old, affords you the time to reflect on issues that get obscured or repressed during those years you are too busy living the life. We can put the realization out of our mind, pretend it doesn't exist, or like some, hope they are exempt for the inevitable. But the certainty of impending death is inescapable.

We spend much of our life, not living in the present, but thinking about, and planning for later. The living of this minute, day, or week, is often postponed or delayed, when it can be rescheduled for a time of enjoyment. The daily grind of life often forces us to live for tomorrow, and just try to get through today.

However, life is short, and you only get to live each moment once. There are no replay buttons, or rewind. Although we must carry our past forward, we must ensure that each moment provides us with more than a plan for the future. Each day is precious and we must allow for each of the moments that shape what is to come. But, happiness cannot be saved for another day.

So what does one do? How do we encompass our now, knowing what the future holds. I have always believed that moments of joy and contentment should be savored. They should be stored in a special place in our mind, where they can extracted, and re-enjoyed, when life isn't going so well. These moments of happiness can be used like a sedative to calm and soothe the soul and rejuvenate the spirit.

I also believe that today should not always be traded for tomorrow. We must be responsible for our destiny, and ensure that we progress in life in a positive manner. But those obligations should not obscure, or burden the enjoyment, of today.

Today is real, and is here now. There is always a possibility that tomorrow will not come to fruition Of course, I am not suggesting that you should merely live for today, and ignore tomorrow. I have prepared for my later years with the usual requirements for sustaining my lifestyle. I have shared my life with others, and others have shared theirs with me. This has required that we all give up something for another. But it does not require that you give up all.

I have lived life to the fullest, given the restraints that have stood in my way. Life does not come with a set of instructions. Sometimes you feel your way along, like traveling in the dark without a light. Use all your senses, and most of all, enjoy your life each and every day, as it may be your last. I truly believe that you should live well, love much, and laugh often. After all, death is always just around the corner for those who live.

# About the Author

John D. McCann is a true advocate of self-reliance. Having been expired by John Burroughs, he started writing essays many years ago in regard to his thoughts and views of nature, living, and self-reliance. This is his first book of essays whereby he describes his views and thoughts in a manner that is not only introspective and thought provoking, but often uses his words to paint a descriptive picture of his reflections, views, and feelings.

John D. McCann is a true advocate of self-reliance. He practices the skills and works at a self-reliant lifestyle. He dislikes the term "Expert" and considers himself a student of self-reliance, survival, and emergency preparedness. He continues in his endeavor to learn and practice the skills necessary to enhance his knowledge and abilities.

John is the author of three previous books, "Practical Self-Reliance - Reducing Your Dependency On Others," "Build the Perfect Survival Kit," now in its 2nd Edition, and "Stay Alive! Survival Skills You Need." He has written dozens of articles and has been published in "Field and Stream," "Wilderness Way," where he was featured on the cover, "Self-Reliance Illustrated," and "Survival Quarterly Magazine." He has appeared on the "Martha Stewart Show" teaching how to build a survival kit. He also has various YouTube videos teaching skills.

He is the founder and owner of Survival Resources, a company that designs and builds custom survival kits, and sells products related to survival and emergency preparedness. He can be contacted at SurvivalResources.com

# Other Books By The Author

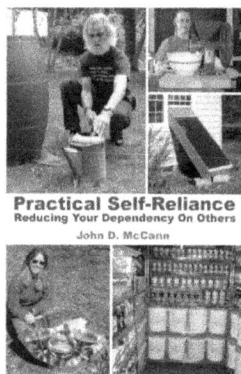

***Build the Perfect Survival Kit*** is the first book ever written exclusively on building survival kits. It was published by Krause Publication (now KP Books), April, 2005. It was so successful that the publisher asked that he do a 2nd, Expanded and Revised Edition. It has a new Forward by Christopher Nyerges. With major additions to the components section and new chapters on Cookware & Stoves, Modifying Your Gear, Everyday Carry & Get-Home Bags, and Evacuation Kits & Bug-Out Bags. The 2nd Edition is 30% larger than the original.

***Stay Alive! - Survival Skills You Need:*** Having a survival kit is not enough - You must know what to do with it! Armed with the techniques in ***Stay Alive! Survival Skills You Need***, you will be prepared to survive. Building on the essentials presented in his first book, ***Build the Perfect Survival Kit***, author John D. McCann details the survival mentality required to survive common emergencies, then goes on to explain the component skill categories that you must execute to stay alive. With more than 250 pages, 300 full-color photos, and a Foreword by Dave Canterbury, ***Stay Alive! - Survival Skills***

*You Need* provides clear, detailed solutions for surviving emergencies during adventure, sport and travel.

***Practical Self-Reliance - Reducing Your Dependency On Others***: Whether you live in the city, suburbs, or country, you can practice self-reliant methods of living. This book is an in depth look at practical ways you can reduce your dependency on others, and work towards a life of self-reliance. It includes sections on obtaining, preserving, storing, and preparing food, recycling and repurposing, skills and tools of the trade for self-reliance, getting out of debt, the importance of water, lighting and alternative power, sanitation and hygiene, staying warm and cool, transportation options, and more. For anyone who wants to work towards being self-reliant, this book, with over 250 photos and diagrams, offers many helpful suggestions and ideas.

Signed copies of all three of these books are available at SurvivalResources.com. They are also available at Amazon.com and wherever fine books are sold.